Dear Peter Pan...

CATHERINE HAILL

Dear Peter Pan...

FOREWORD BY
NANETTE NEWMAN

THEATRE MUSEUM
VICTORIA AND ALBERT MUSEUM

Published by the Victoria and Albert Museum, London
First published 1983
© Crown copyright

ISBN 0 905209 51 6

Introduction by Catherine Haill
Foreword by Nanette Newman © Bryan Forbes Ltd
Design by Patrick Yapp
Photography by Hugh Sainsbury
Photoset by Southern Positives and Negatives (SPAN), Lingfield, Surrey
Printed in the Netherlands by drukkerij de Lange/van Leer BV

FRONT COVER: Detail from the poster advertising the original
production of *Peter Pan*, Duke of York's Theatre, 27 December 1904.
Colour lithograph by Charles Buchel.

BACK COVER: Wendy gives Peter a kiss. Colour postcard from a
watercolour by Barham.

FRONTISPIECE: J. M. Barrie, *c.* 1890. Photographer unknown.

Contents

Introduction

By the time that *Peter Pan, or, The Boy Who Wouldn't Grow Up* was first produced in London, at the Duke of York's Theatre on 27 December 1904, its author J.M. Barrie was already a well-established novelist and dramatist. Born in Scotland in 1860, Barrie had begun his career as a journalist after graduating from Edinburgh University in 1882. In 1885 he came to London, hoping that journalism would provide a regular income while he fulfilled his ambitions as a novelist. Six years later his third novel, *The Little Minister*, was acclaimed as 'a Book of Genius', and more successful novels and plays soon followed. By 1902 when Barrie's plays *Quality Street* and *The Admirable Crichton* were first produced in London, one critic even noted that an audience only had to see the curtain rise on a play by Barrie to fall into a contented purring! Barrie himself was always far less sanguine about the popularity of his plays, once writing gloomily to a friend: 'When a man dramatises, his troubles begin.'

Barrie had good reason to be uncertain of the reception of *Peter Pan* since it was unlike any play he had written before. Indeed, it was unlike any play *anyone* had ever written! It required an enormous cast, contained the most improbable and fantastic scenes and events, and above all, needed a great amount of stage machinery to achieve the complicated technical effects. When Barrie finished writing the first draft of the play in April 1904 he realised the difficulties of staging it and decided to read it to the actor-manager Herbert Beerbohm Tree whose lavish productions at His Majesty's Theatre were renowned. After hearing the first two acts of *Peter and Wendy*, as it was then called, Tree decided

Nina Boucicault as Peter Pan in the original production, Duke of York's Theatre, 27 December 1904. Photograph by Ellis & Walery.

that Barrie had gone mad and begged him to stop. Years later when asked why he had rejected the play, Tree replied: 'God knows, and I have promised to tell no-one else.' At the time, however, Tree was so sure of his decision that he immediately wrote to Barrie's friend, the American producer Charles Frohman, to advise him of his apparent insanity:

> Barrie has gone out of his mind. .... I am sorry to say it, but you ought to know it. He's just read me a play. He's going to read it to you, so I am warning you. I know I have not gone woozy in my mind, because I have tested myself since hearing the play, but Barrie must be mad.

Frohman came to London at the end of April and when Barrie read his 'mad' script to him the producer was absolutely delighted. As Denis Mackail wrote in his biography of Barrie:

> Frohman never hesitated about it. .... The magic which would grip millions had called to him already, even from ninety pages of typescript. He would never get over it if he couldn't present this play.

Frohman's immediate reaction was of complete confidence in both play and playwright and he undertook to back it at any expense, giving instructions that Barrie should have everything he wanted for the production at his theatre, the Duke of York's: 'No half-measures, never mind the risk.' The title of the play was changed to *Peter Pan* and Dion Boucicault was chosen as director. A company of fifty was engaged and William Nicholson was commissioned to design the costumes. Mr Crook was asked to compose suitable music. Dances were to be arranged by Willie Warde. George Kirby's Flying Ballet Company was approached to produce less cumbersome 'flying' equipment than had ever been used before on the stage, and the first Peter and Wendy – Nina Boucicault and Hilda Trevelyan – were initiated into the hazardous secrets of stage flight, along with the first John and Michael, to be played by George Hersee and Winifred Geoghegan.

Hilda Trevelyan as Wendy in the original production, Duke of York's Theatre, 27 December 1904. Photograph by Ellis & Walery.

During the difficult rehearsal period of *Peter Pan*, Barrie must have come to doubt his own sanity in conceiving the piece. He watched chaotic rehearsals and patiently re-wrote whole scenes, adding new lines to fill the technically enforced gaps in the action. Although the cast had been sworn to secrecy about the play, fantastic rumours had leaked to the press and critics were impatient to see Mr Barrie's marvellous new production. The first night was announced as 22 December but by mid-December the mechanism for raising the Little House to the tree tops was not ready, nor was the method for installing a heavy set in the third act. The complicated ideas of a flying eagle that could lift Hook across the stage were abandoned, as was that of Tinker Bell being played by an actress moving on stage behind a giant reducing lens. The collapse of a lift and the consequent loss of scenery finally enforced the postponement of the first night, and Barrie spent that Christmas re-writing the ending for the fifth time. Against all odds, *Peter Pan* opened on 27 December 1904, and Peter, Wendy, Michael and John embarked on the first of their many trips to the Never-Never Land. Much of Barrie's writing contained autobiographical elements, but perhaps no other work was ever so close to his heart. The play *Peter Pan* resulted from his friendship with the Llewelyn-Davies family, which assumed a lifelong importance for him. Married to Mary Ansell but childless, Barrie loved children and had the innate knack of communicating with them. Adults would often find an interview with Barrie a terrifying experience, but children immediately made him their confidant. As one actress recalled who first met Barrie when she was eight years old:

> We came to look on Mr Barrie as our friend ... he was our companion. When we were away from him he seemed to be with us; he was more present than our parents ...

The story of *Peter Pan* grew from stories that Barrie made up with the Llewelyn-Davies boys, the first of whom he met in 1897. Barrie lived near Kensington Gardens and on walks with his St Bernard dog, Porthos, he made the acquaintance of the five-year old George, the four-year old Jack, and the baby Peter Llewelyn-Davies, with their nanny in the Gardens. Barrie wove adventure stories for the boys on these meetings and over the next few years

Statue of Peter Pan in Kensington Gardens, by Sir George Frampton.
Commissioned by Barrie, and erected 1912.

he wove the boys into his writing. On 31 December 1897 Barrie
met the boys' mother at a dinner party and found her as captivating
as her children. Sylvia Llewelyn-Davies, the daughter of the
author George Du Maurier and the sister of the actor Gerald Du
Maurier, obviously found conversation with Barrie easier than
others did and for Barrie this meeting confirmed his friendship
with the family. He began to meet the children more regularly,

11

often visiting them at their house, and although Sylvia's husband Arthur may have been annoyed by these visits from a self-appointed 'uncle', there was nothing in the relationship to which he could object. His wife's friendship with the rather unprepossessing but eminent author was clearly platonic; his children loved this funny short gentleman who told them stories and wiggled his eyebrows and ears. The friendship and the inventive tales flourished, Barrie's own flights of fancy being enriched by the childrens' imagination. Ideas for a novel based on the fantasies took shape in Barrie's mind, but the first record of the stories that he issued was a privately printed edition of two copies of a book called *The Boy Castaways of Black Lake Island* 'being a record of the terrible adventures of the brothers Davies in the summer of 1901.'

By this time there was a fourth brother, Michael, born in 1900, and in the summer of 1902 Barrie published his novel *The Little White Bird*. This 'whimsical, sentimental, profound, ridiculous' book had grown from his inventions with the Llewelyn-Davies boys, and featured a character called Peter Pan. In November 1904 the Llewelyn-Davies family was completed by the birth of a fifth son to Sylvia, Nicholas. Barrie's play opened in December and he included Nicholas when he stated later: 'I made Peter by rubbing the five of you violently together, as savages with two sticks produce a flame.'

The critics who had waited anxiously for the first night of *Peter Pan* were not disappointed. Reviewing 'Mr Barrie's Peter Pan-Tomime' one critic declared:

> The piece which last night kept a crowded audience at the Duke of York's in ecstasies is less a play than a playground. A playground in which Mr Barrie's impish sense of fun may disport itself to the fullest.

Another wrote:

> *Peter Pan* is not so much a play as a spree, and never has Mr Barrie spreed to better purpose. The reception at every stage was enthusiastic ... Mr Barrie loves children, and none other can so well reproduce the charm of childhood on the stage.

Barrie's 'marvellous fertility in humorous and pathetic touches'
were praised, as were the actors. 'Miss Nina Boucicault is excellent
as Peter ... Miss Hilda Trevelyan is most delightful and sympathetic as Wendy ... Nana, as acted by Mr Arthur Lupino is
much funnier than any performing dog can be ... Mr Gerald Du
Maurier is amusing as Mr Darling and convulsing as the treble-
dyed villain Hook ... Miss Dorothea Baird makes a sweet and
sympathetic Mrs Darling ... Messrs George Shelton and Sydney
Harcourt are very droll as two pirates, and Miss Pauline Chase

13

dances bewitchingly, especially when she encases her feet in two pillows.'

The first-night audience were eager captives of Barrie's world. They clapped wildly to revive Tinker Bell and loved the flying and the fighting, the crocodile and the clock. The applause when the curtain fell reassured everybody concerned that their efforts had been worthwhile. The public loved Barrie's 'insanity' and a telegram was immediately despatched to the anxious Charles Frohman in New York:

Peter Pan all right. Looks like a big success.

But for all the fulsome praise of the critics Barrie's favourite reaction to his play was that of a child who had been given a seat in the author's own box. When asked which bit of the play the child liked best, he replied:

What I *think* I liked best was tearing up the programme and dropping the bits on people's heads.

Barrie's play had evolved with children and when they were not tearing up their programmes but involved in the action it appealed directly to them. The story had come from the real dreams of children – to fly, to live in a secret place, to fight the 'baddies' and win – and from the first performance children in the audience believed in the characters and wanted to write and ask them questions. Pauline Chase, whose performance in the original production as the First Twin had been noted by critics, was given the part of Peter for the third production in 1906. She continued to play Peter for the next eight years and received hundreds of letters from children asking her about life in the Never-Never Land. Even Michael Llewelyn-Davies wrote to Pauline Chase in 1906:

Dear Peter Pan

thank you very much For the Post Card you Gave me I am Longing for some more of them and I have sent you A picture of the little House For you and Nick-o thinks he can fly. But he Only tumbles about he send his love

From Michael.

George Shelton as Smee, the part he played from the first production, 1904, until his retirement, 1930. Postcard from a photograph by Morrison's Studios.

Most of the children who wrote to Pauline Chase thought that she would have noticed them in the theatre when they shouted out or clapped, and some asked logical questions:

Dear Peter Pan

You say that every time somebody says 'I dont believe in fairys a fairy dies, so would you please tell me if every time somebody says 'I believe in fairys' a fairy comes?

And another had obviously understood the need for regular meal times when she wrote to Peter:

will you please come and see me in bed, And take me to Never Never Land, but bring me back in time for Brekfist.

In 1909 Pauline Chase published a selection of the letters she had received as Peter, noting the fact that although she and Wendy always received a lot of correspondence from children, so did Smee (played by George Shelton), who was part of the Pirate gang:

Wendy and I are sometimes rather jealous of Smee, who is surely the best loved of all wicked people. He says scarcely a word in the play of which he ought not to be ashamed, and he makes (or thinks he makes) the most horrifying faces, but this does not in the least affect the love of children for him; they seem to regard him as a dear old misguided creature whose heart is in the right place whatever he says or does, and they write daily asking him to come to tea and bring the sewing machine.

We do not know what became of the originals of these letters to Peter Pan as played by Pauline Chase, but in 1982 the Theatre Museum was given a collection of letters sent to another Peter, Miss Eva Embury. She played Peter for several years on tour in England during the First World War. She kept all the letters written to her by children, along with postcards and photographs of various productions of the play and the wooden 'pan-pipes' she used on stage. Her collection reveals how much she enjoyed the play and the part of Peter Pan. The letters show how she replied to the children, sent them presents and entertained them to tea. There must be many who still remember seeing Eva Embury play Peter or even writing some of these letters. They have now grown up, but like Peter Pan, their letters remain eternally young.

Catherine Haill

Eva Embury as Peter Pan which she played on tour *c.* 1918.
Photograph by Bertram Park.

Foreword

From the moment *Peter Pan* was first presented to the public, audiences have never ceased to be enchanted by Barrie's little boy who refused to grow up. At the time of its first production in 1904 it was said it required *the most stupendous courage and confidence to put on a play that, from the manuscript, sounded like a combination of circus and extravaganza – a play in which children flew in and out of rooms, crocodiles swallowed alarm clocks, a man exchanged places with a dog in a kennel, and various other absurd and ridiculous things happened.*

Like many of Barrie's works, it had a curious genesis. The acting out of the play came before the writing of it. Barrie was fascinated (some might say obsessed) with the four sons of Sylvia and Arthur Llewelyn-Davies. He thought of himself as the surrogate father to them, and for their part they enjoyed a friendship with a man of genius who could enchant them with his fantasies. Through him they were constantly led through an exciting land of make-believe. And the relationship was not entirely one-sided, since Barrie enjoyed a tame and adoring audience – a perfect sounding-board, as it were, for the stories that eventually shaped themselves into *Peter Pan*. If one is looking for a reason for the perennial success of the play, it perhaps lies in the fact that it began as a labour of love, tried out in private on the age group for whom it was intended. From the games he invented for and the stories he told to the Davies boys, Barrie gradually shaped the final play, and perhaps without that captive audience of four he might never have written it.

Over the years many critics have attempted to analyse the secret of the enduring success of *Peter Pan*, and it would be foolish to

Robb Harwood as Captain Hook in the third revival of *Peter Pan*, Duke of York's Theatre, 17 December 1907. Reproduced from *The Sketch*, 29 January 1908.

pretend that it has not had its detractors. I think the nearest one can get to discovering why it has continued to captivate children and adults alike over eight decades, is that Barrie understood, as few before or since, the workings of a child's imagination. He turned all the accepted rules inside out. To start with, nearly every child longs to grow up: indeed, aren't we always saying to children 'you must wait until you're older before you can do that' or 'you mustn't say that until you're grown up.' Therefore, to the majority of children, this carrot of being grown-up, constantly dangled before their eyes, becomes in a sense a 'never-never' land over the horizon – a place where *they* will make the rules, and where *they* will be able to do what *they* wish without always being told. Aren't most of the games children play based on pretending to be grown up – Mothers and Fathers, Train Drivers, Doctors, Nurses?

Now Barrie, very cleverly, turned this idea on its head and gave us a little boy hero who *didn't* want to grow up. Peter makes his audiences believe that staying a child is more fun, that being grown up is not the blissful state that adults maintain it is, but is really a time of responsibility. Barrie gave to Peter the magical power that most children long for, whether it be going to the moon, or being Superman! Peter could actually fly. He was also brave and cheeky and capable of inspiring love, as in the case of Wendy, without being mawkish. But then Barrie hit upon yet another unusual twist: he made the Father a rather childish character, someone who could be wrong – a quite titillating idea for a child at the turn of the century. Again, Nana, the dog, was bestowed with many human qualities, and instead of having a conventional fairy, he invented one who was naughty and capable of being jealous while at the same time highly vulnerable should anybody not believe in her.

Barrie's unique powers are never more in evidence than in the scene where Tinkerbell, the fairy, is threatened. Anyone who has ever looked around a rapt audience at the moment when Peter steps down to the footlights and pleads for everybody to clap hands if they believe in fairies so that Tinker Bell can live, will have seen a sea of enraptured faces. It is a moment that remains in one's heart long after the final curtain.

Arthur Lupino as Nana in the original production, Duke of York's Theatre, 27 December 1904. Drawing by Ralph Cleaver, reproduced from *The Sketch*, 4 January 1905.

Yet Barrie still has other tricks up his sleeve. He gives the accepted conventions yet another twist, giving the child who longs for adventure an all-important safety-belt by making Wendy the 'mother figure'. Wendy is sane and sensible, knowing that one day she will be a proper mother, but for the moment instead of having dolls she has the Lost Boys, pretend children of her own to care for. Combined with all this Barrie superimposes first love, love in its purest sense, between Peter and Wendy. And surrounding the central figures he has pirates, mermaids, wolves, Redskins, crocodiles; he has the building of the little house, the Never-Never land, and finally a happy, sad ending. The blend is masterly, measured and presented with a sure-fire panache that ensures that the whole is a banquet fit to set before any child, and which will be devoured with wondrous relish.

If we turn now to the selection of letters in this volume, we can see how completely Barrie's magic works. Children accept Peter totally. From the security of their theatre seats they surrender themselves to Barrie's fantasies, believing everything they see without question. They close their minds to the fact that Peter is being played by an actress (often of mature years). To them Nana is a real dog, Peter does fly through the nursery window, the crocodile does swallow the alarm clock, Tinker Bell could die if they don't clap their hands. These letters from the past could be duplicated a thousand times over from succeeding generations of young theatregoers, and I find the fragile innocence of the beliefs expressed very touching.

21

I remember when my own daughters saw *Peter Pan* for the first time they came away utterly convinced that they, too, could fly. We had a great deal of leaping off the bed accompanied by shrieks of 'I can fly' followed by the inevitable thud of a crashed landing. Repeated failures never seemed to deter them. Sarah, our eldest daughter, actually wrote to Peter asking if he could find time to give her some flying lessons, stating she would be 'most grateful'. Emma, on the other hand, longed for Peter to fly in through her bedroom window, although courage always failed her at the last moment and she insisted that the window was bolted.

I was recently working with an actor who related his first experience of going to the theatre and falling in love simultaneously. Taken at age four to see *Peter Pan* he immediately fell desperately in love with Wendy. He was in a stage box, he told me, dressed in a little velvet suit, and suddenly leapt to his feet, threw out his arms and shouted: 'Wendy, Wendy, I love you, come home to tea' and had a sharp smack for his pains which swiftly curtailed his passion and his theatregoing!

Tinker Bell represents the magical force that many children long to have. I know of one little girl who always extricated herself from scrapes by saying 'It wasn't me, I didn't do that, it was that naughty Tinkerbell'. But although the supporting characters in the play are so important to the whole, it is Peter himself who claims the final adoration. He is forever. He is the rebel, the exception to the mould, the enviable one who cocks a snoot at rules and regulations and gets away with it. Perhaps in so many ways he is a small part of all of us – the part that we are often afraid to admit exists: the still small voice crying out for a return to a Never-Never land where the innocence and joy of childhood remains untouched. Reading these letters I am reminded of my own lost beliefs and I remember how, for a short spell in a darkened auditorium, I too surrendered to the genius of Barrie.

Nanette Newman

Cissie Loftus as Peter Pan in the first revival, Duke of York's Theatre, 19 December 1905. Postcard from a photograph by Ellis & Walery.

Some of the members of the
cast of the original production,
Duke of York's Theatre,
27 December 1904. Drawings
by Ralph Cleaver reproduced
from *The Sketch*,
4 January 1905.

OPPOSITE Eva Embury, *c.*1918.
Postcard, from a
photograph by Alex Corbett.

Pauline Chase as First Twin

Hilda Trevelyan as Wendy

Winifred Geoghegan as Michael

Ela Q. May as Liza

George Hersee as John

Miriam Nesbitt as Tiger Lily

Sydney Harcourt as Gentleman Starkey

Acknowledgements

This book has been compiled from the letters and photographs that belonged to the actress Eva Embury. She died in 1981, having kept these mementoes carefully for over sixty years. She knew the author of *Peter Pan*, J. M. Barrie, and loved the part of Peter that he had created. Thanks are due to her friend, Miss Olive Davies, who brought the letters and photographs to the Theatre Museum, as Miss Embury had wished before her death. As Miss Davies said: 'Eva embodied the Peter Pan spirit all her life, being full of zest and excitement in everything she did. She would have been thrilled to know that this book was to be published.'

We would also like to thank the writers of all these letters to Miss Embury, whom we have been unable to trace, but who may be reminded of their childish handwriting and have vivid memories of meeting and seeing Peter Pan.

We are most grateful to Miss Nanette Newman for providing the foreword to this book.

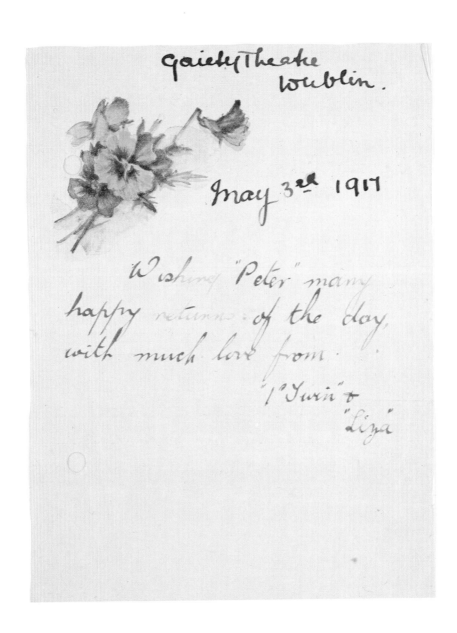

Gaiety Theatre
Dublin.

May 3rd 1917

Wishing "Peter" many
happy returns of the day,
with much love from.
"Twin" &
"Liza"

Eva Embury as Peter Pan which she played on tour *c.*1918.
Photograph by Wrather & Buys.

Our Lady's School
Tooling S.W
18. 3. 18.

Dear Peter Pan
            I am writing this little
letter, to thank you for sending as
the tickets I enjoyed myself very much
so did every body else I think.
        Why don't you want to grow up I would
like know to very much. Please Peter Pan will
you ask the fairies (because I beleive in Fairies)
to send me a mouth organ like you
have so that when I blow it you
the faires will come + dance for me
I like dancing very much. I like
Wendie very much she had I
very nice nurse it was a shame
for Mr Darling to shut him in
a kennel. I would like to fly like

you. Was not Michael a naughty boy not to take his medicine   I am glad we all clapped when you said "Do you beleive in Fairies" or it would have been a sham if Tinker Bell had died.

I think that is all now. I wish you the best of luck

from your affectionat little friend

Dorothy Kerwin

X X X

Eva Embury as Peter Pan which she played on tour *c.* 1918
Postcard, from a photograph by Rita Martin.

13 Tabor Grove
Wimbledon
S.W. 19.

My dear Peter Pan,
                    I went to see you last
night & I just loved you & the play. I liked it a
great deal more than the Pantomime we had
here. I wish I was acting in Peter Pan' with you; I
was on in Brer Rabbit & and Mr Fox' at Brighton
this year and I had a lovely time. Will you please
write something in my autograph book. & will you
ask Wendy & John & Michael to write also. I
hope I shall see you again sometime.
                    I must close now
                         with love and x x x
                         from Rhoda Rivers

The Darling family. Act 3, scene 3 from the original
production, Duke of York's Theatre, 27 December 1904.
Dorothea Baird and Gerald Du Maurier as Mr and Mrs Darling,
Hilda Trevelyan as Wendy, George Hersee and Winifred Geoghegan
as John and Michael, with Arthur Lupino as Nana.
Reproduced from a contemporary magazine.

7/4/18

Dear Peter

Just a little note to day how sorry I am because you could not com to tea to-day I did so want to see you

I am going to see "Peter Pan" when you play "Peter" in town, we will all be to see you fly.

With lots of love & kisses from Joseph and Theodore

x x x x , x x x .

Programme cover illustration for the third revival
of *Peter Pan*, Duke of York's Theatre, 16 December 1907.
Designed by John Hassall.

dear Peter, please tell me
how to fly. come at 12 oclock
please, at night, I have tried
but I cannot manage it. how is
Hook getting on in his crocodile.
how is Michael getting on with
his summing in air, and
how is mr. Miserable Starkey
is he still still so miserable
as he was when I saw him
last. Is the clock still run
down.
    Love from Jean M Matheson

55 Wheatland Drive
    Lanark

FALKIRK
8. — M
7 FEB 18

FALKI
8. 1 M
7 FEB 18

POSTAGE ✶ REVENUE
ONE PENNY

*Master Peter Pan.
Kings Theatre.
Glasgow
W.*

The crocodile approaches Captain Hook.
Scene from Act 2 in the original production
of *Peter Pan*, Duke of York's Theatre,
27 December 1904. Reproduced from a
contemporary magazine.

35 Ardgown st Greenock

Dear Peter Pan. I would love
if you would give me
Johns wire. for I would
love to fly.
if you can send a note.
I saw ~~you~~ at the Kings
theatre. you were so good
love to Wendy. Michael and
John. with love.

from Margot Webb.

look over the paper xxxxxx
xxx

Dear Peter Pan.

Kitty Love
54 Brougham
Greenock

I would just Love if you would
would
give me a wire. so. would
you give me a wire.

please do. for I do

want to fly. your

wire please. I was at the

Kings theatre on wednes-
day and you were the
best   I saw your wire
with Love from Kitty x x x x x

Kitty Love
54 Brougham St
Greenock

23 Fitzwilliam Square
Dublin

"Over the Hills..."

My dear Peter Pan

Mother is writing this
for me because I have
been very ill & had an
operation. I am only
five & have a book
all about you, &
Nannie & Mummie
promised to bring me

to see you whenever
you came to Dublin
& now instead of going
I have to lie in bed.
& Dear Peter Pan I love
you so very much. Will
you come soon soon
again to Dublin & let
me see you. I love
the fairies too, & my
Mummie was once
a fairy & was called
fairy Silverwing, & sh

the children used to get
her to tell them all about
Fairyland.
　　"Please dear "Peter
Pan" write me a little
letter if you have time.
I give my love to
"Wendy." Good bye
Love & kisses from
　　Your loving friend
　　　　Desirée"
"dear "Peter Pan""
The above was written

S.1337-1982

by me at Desirée's dictation
& I send it to you unaltered
She has been very ill &
has to lie for some months
She loves "Peter Pan"
but has been so good
about the disappointment
of not seeing the play.
With every good wish
for a successful week
　　Yours sincerely
　　Elspeth de Courcy to Bell
Desirée insists on this
love duck being sent to
you!

Dorothea Baird as Mrs Darling
in the original production,
Duke of York's Theatre,
27 December 1904. Drawing
by Ralph Cleaver, reproduced
from *The Sketch*, 4 January 1905.

11 Kelvin Drive.
Kelvinside
Glasgow

Wednesday

My dear "Peter Pan".
Thanks so much for the sweet photographs, it is just too adorable of you to be so kind. We miss "Peter" most awfully in Glasgow, and wish you would make Glasgow "the never, never land"; and we'll come & join your band
Thanking you ever so much again
Yours Sincerely
Aileen Dick
Judy Thomson.

The lost boys with Wendy. Act 2, scene 1,
from the original production, Duke of
York's Theatre, 27 December 1904.
Nina Boucicault as Peter and Hilda
Trevelyan as Wendy. Reproduced from
the *Peter Pan Keepsake*, edited by
W. T. Stead, 1907.

217 Church St
Walker

Dear Miss Embury

I expect you
will think I am awfully
cheeky. but my little boy and
girl have tormented my
life out all this week end to
bring them to see "peter pan"
on Wednesday. and as I
cannot afford the 2/8 it would
cost for gallery and car fare (I
would have to pay for baby too)
I thought that perhaps you
might be so kind as to send
a pass to let them see you.
the last time the play was
here. we waited for nearly 2
hours. then it was full early
door and I promised them then
the next time it came I
would take them and I cannot
keep my promise. you see Miss
their father is "somewhere in.
France in the 7th Border Regt.
and that not being a local.
Regt they miss all the treats
that the Tyneside Scottish and
Irish have had. they are only
6 and 8 years old. hoping you
will grant me this favour

I remain yours sincerely

Mary Alexander
217 Church St
Walker

P.S. I have never asked anything in my life before. and I have lived in this house for nearly 12 years. My landlord can speak for my respectability.

M. A.

Men of the Border Regiment resting in a front line trench, Thiepvale Wood, August 1916. Photograph reproduced by courtesy of the Imperial War Museum.

217 Church
St
Walker

Dear Miss Embury

I thank you very
much indeed for your
Kindness, in giving us
such a delightful treat today
we all enjoyed ourselves.
I never expected you to
treat me too. and you left.
is a too much but I bought cakes
for the children with it.. I will
never do such a thing again
as I worried myself so much
when I posted the letter to

I would willingly of taken
back again. as I thought it u
a most forward thing to do.
but Oh! what a torment my
mind was in till I got ya
Kind letter. and if it mak
the giver any happier than
the reciever. you should be
very happy. for the children
think that you are a Kind
Fairy to them. so wishing yo
the best of Health to Keep o
making people happy. and w
best of luck. I remain your

Mrs Alexand

The departure of the little Darlings for the Never-Never Land. Drawing by Ralph Cleaver of the original production, Duke of York's Theatre, 27 December 1904. Reproduced from *The Sketch*, 4 January 1905.

Dear Peter Pan.

I saw you flying today and I would like to be able to fly also. Mother says only fairies fly I wish I knew Tinker Bell I shouted out that I believed in fairies so that Tinker Bell would get better I liked you very much and both Elsie and I were sorry when it was over we could sit all night watching you. Mother says I have to thank you nicely for giving Elsie and I such a nice treat and if daddy is home when you come back I will bring him to see you so good-night

and God bless you I send you a few kisses for my sister Elsie and

yours truly
Freddy.
Alexander

x x x x x x x x x x x

P.S. I hope you wont mind Freddy thanking you too. Elsie wanted to write too but I think you will have trouble enough to make all that is here out

M. A.

34 merr
crescent
off
Gosforth

My Dear Peter.
Thank - you very much for
your letter and photo
I hope when you come back
to newcastle. You will come
and have tea with me.
with love and kisses
    from Rosamond Lynn

XXXXXXX XXXXXXX
XXXXXXXX XXXXX
XXXXXXXXX XXX
XXXXXXXX XXXXXX
XXXXXXXXXXXXX

Peter Pan
Theatre
Royal
Portsmouth

ABOVE Phillip Tonge as Michael in *Peter Pan* which he played in Manchester, Christmas 1906. Postcard.

LEFT Walter Cross as John in *Peter Pan* which he played in Manchester, Christmas 1906. Postcard.

34 Moor
cresant
Gosforth

my Dear Peter Pan.
I came to see you yester-day
and I engoyed it very much much.
and there is one thing I want
to ask you and that is
how do you fly I want
to learn here. please write
soon and tell me. I am nine
years old. and I have got
a pug dog
I send my love and
x x s from
Rosamond Lynn

XXXX XXXXXXX X
XXXX XXXXXXX X

Peter Pan teaching Wendy, Michael and John
to fly. Illustration by Charles Buchel of the
original production, Duke of York's Theatre,
27 December 1904. Reproduced from a
contemporary magazine.

37 Chesnut Grove
Birkenhead
March 14th

Dear Peter Pan

I received your photograph this morning. I do love it, and I do think is was good of you to send

I had a letter from Smee last Thursday. I was sorry he wasn't here this time. Last time he came, he came out to see us.

I have a lovely book of the music of Peter Pan, and my favourite bits are the treetops and the Fairy House, although I love the music of the lagoon scene. I have in a kind of way grown up with Peter Pan, I have known the music and story since I was tiny. I think it gets sadder as you get older. I know I cried this last time. Thanking you again. I remain your Very Sincerely

Margaret Seward.

LEFT George Shelton as Smee in the original production, Duke of York's Theatre, 27 December 1904. Drawing by Ralph Cleaver, reproduced from *The Sketch*, 4 January 1905.

OPPOSITE Rosamund Bury and Geraldine Wilson as the Mermaid and the Baby Mermaid in the Lagoon scene. This was added to the first revival of *Peter Pan* as Act 3. Duke of York's Theatre, 19 December 1905.

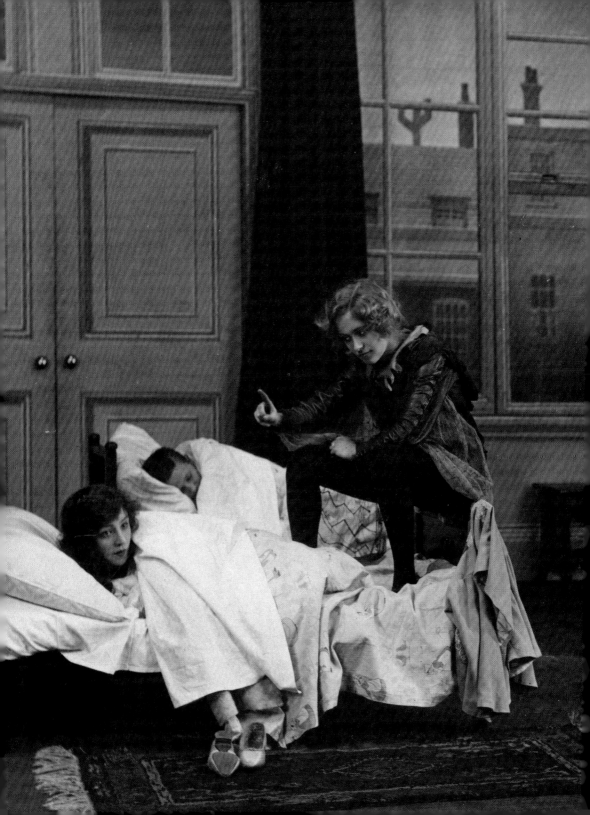

Dear Tinkerbell
will you ge*
blow some
fairy dust
over me to
make me fly.
Love from
Kathleen
Chapman

12 Foster Road
Alverstoke

OPPOSITE Peter Pan visits the children in the Nursery. Pauline Chase as Peter, Hilda Trevelyan as Wendy and Herbert Hollom as Michael. Duke of York's Theatre, 17 December 1907.

OVERLEAF Poster advertising the original production of *Peter Pan*, Duke of York's Theatre, 27 December 1904. Colour lithograph by Charles Buchel, 1904.

CHAS·A·BUCHEL·1904

41 Burke Street,
Bilton,
Harrogate,

Dear Miss Embury,

I saw you in "Peter Pan" on Wednesday afternoon, and I liked you so much that I wished to write to you. I saw your photographs hanging outside the theatre and I thought I would write and ask you for one. Were you "Peter Pan" about three years ago? Because I saw it then and I thought it would be the same company, as the little maid was the author then. I would so like to see you off the stage, so if you have time before you leave Harrogate will you come and see me at Stewarts, in Beulah Street, which is quite near the theatre, for as you must know I am fourteen and at work. I have a friend called Ethel Ward and she is dark like Wendy. It is funny how there are two people named the same. Do you know Rita Moya or Eva Ellis? for I have written to them and they sent me their photographs, so I have quite a collection of actresses, both Film and the other sort, I don't know what to call them. I have a great longing to be an actress, but my parents flatly refuse, so my only consolation is writing to actresses. When I tell my mother I've written to you, she'll say I can't go to see a play, without falling in love with somebody. Of course my parents don't mind me being on a local stage but as for making it a proffession, she'd see me dead first. She doesn't mind me becoming a "cinema star" someday but I'd much rather be behind the footlights. By the way, just before I close I want to ask you if you know Winifred Roma? She stayed at my auntie's once and she is so lovely.

I am afraid I shall have to close now with much love from

Freda Simms.

x x x x x x x x x x x x x x x x x x

P.S. Please come and see me or please write to me.

x x x x x x x x x x x x x x y

Eva Embury as Peter Pan which she played on tour *c.*1918.
Postcard, from a photograph by Bertram Park.

28/12/24

Mayfield
Biggin Hill
Westerham
Kent.

Dear Peter Pan
        Thank you so much for
the book, I am just reading it,
I like it very much.
        Santa Claus came and left some
toys but he did not leave any for
me, I expect I am too big now.
        I had heaps of toys.
        I am writing with the fountain
pen which Mummy gave me.
She also gave me a nice pencil and
a pair of goloshes which save
me cleaning my boots.
Daddy gave me a geometry set.
I hope your are enjoying yourself?

Pauline Chase as Peter Pan which she played
annually from the second revival, Duke of
York's Theatre, 18 December 1906, until
the end of the tenth revival in January 1914.
Postcard.

good bye Peter Pan love from
Horace
X Y Y ✳ X X

St Kitts.
Headington.
Oxford.

Dear Peter Pan
            It was perfectly lovely
of you to send me a photograph,
you look so pretty in it, & such
a nice letter. I shall keep them
both always, we had a Children's
Party at home yesterday, of course
I showed them to all my friends
they were so envious, have I spelt
is right? Molly, Ruth, Barbara,
& I are just longing for this
evening to come to see you again
at the Theatre we dont know.

Pauline Chase as Peter Pan which she played
annually from the second revival, Duke of York's
Theatre, 18 December 1906, until the end of the
tenth revival in January 1914. Postcard.

how to thank you nicely enough
for letting us come; Molly & Ruth
are my sisters and Barbara
is a cousin, We call her Babs,
she had never been to a Theatre
before last Thursday she thought
it was lovely I am going to pin
some more apples on to this letter
& leave them for you all this
evening I do hope you nearly
like them, Daddy says you are
going away after this week to
play somewhere else we wish
you were not, but it will be
nice for children who live there,
I wonder where somewhere else is?

We have some big trees in front of
our house with rooks nests in them,
in the spring when there are young
rooks they make such a noise, at night,
Daddy says it is because they have
got into their wrong pyjamas, —
But I think it is when you come to
see them, so next spring I shall
look for you and leave my window
open   With lots & lots of love
        from Betty.

Darling Peter you acted very well will you tell me how to fly. How did you sit in the air? how did you fly on to the mantlepiece? Did you see me in the Dress Circle.

i wore a tusser silk dress. at between two becble girls my name is Kathleen Chapman 12 Foster Road, alverstoke. Love from Kathleen. XXXXXXXXXXX

The fight on the pirate ship. Act 3, scene 1
from the original production, Duke of York's
Theatre, 27 December 1904. Nina Boucicault
as Peter, Hilda Trevelyan as Wendy,
Gerald Du Maurier as Captain Hook.
Reproduced from the *Peter Pan Keepsake*,
edited by W. T. Stead, 1907.

10 Colville mansions
Powis Terrace
, Bayswater W11

Dear Peter Pan
    Thank you for the lovely day
you are gave the. We enjoyed it very much.
and aliways talking about it.
        Thank you for the lovely
clothes and toys you gave us, we
like them very much. It was so kind
of you to bring them
        Paula has gone home and
Carlo and i went to her home with

r her to tea.
good bye peter pan
love from all.
Horace
+ xxtttxxxx

Zena Dare as Peter Pan which she played
in Manchester, Christmas 1906. Postcard,
from a photograph by Foulsham & Banfield.

Baylie House
Hotel
Slough
Bucks
—

My dear Peter
        Thank you
so much fore
the lovely Box of
choclote you sent

us We like them
very much
        goodbye
                lots of
                    love
                        from
                    Mary
                    and
                    Tommy

Madge Titheradge as
Peter Pan which she
played in the tenth
revival, Duke of
York's Theatre,
24 December 1914.
Reproduced from a
contemporary
magazine.

DEAR PETER PAn
        thank you for the
Presents and the lovely tea
party I enjoyed iT very
much.
Yum loved the dolly ~~sle~~ and
slept wiTH iT all night.
~~it~~ i am writing with
your Pencil.   i like
your house.
        Good bye Peter Pan   love From
        Harace
XX++++ ++++++X ++

Postcard, from a watercolour by Barham.

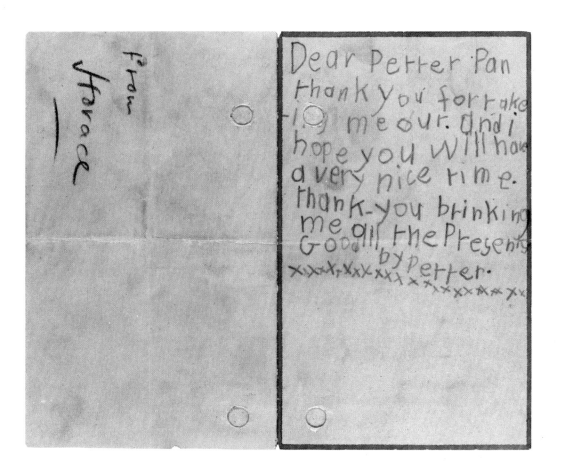

Eva Embury as Peter Pan which she played on tour *c.*1918.
Photograph by Bertram Park.

6 Beaufort Rd
Sheffield

3 March
1st.

My dear Peter,
                I don't
know if you will
recieve this letter
because your letter
was dated 22nd & I did
not recieve it till
Tuesday. Thanks for
your letter & post-card
photograph I mean. It
is the very image of
you. I am very sorry
I am not enclosing
a photograph because
I have not had them

II
taken yet but the next
letter I send I will
enclose one. I was very
delighted when the
letter came for I had
almost given up hope.
I cannot write much
this time as it is ten
past nine & bed-time.
I will write a longer
letter next time. I hope
you recieved this letter.
I have saved your letters
in a letter-case. Well
I shall have to close
now. Much Love &

kisses from
Dorothy
x + + x x+++ +x x
Ⓧ one for "Ink"

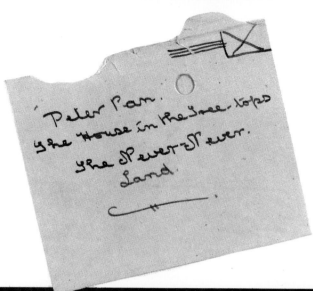

Peter and Wendy with the
house in the treetops.
Pauline Chase as Peter Pan
with Hilda Trevelyan as
Wendy. Duke of York's
Theatre, 17 December 1907.

The Knoll
Neston
        March 21st 16

My dear Peter Pan

        I did so

enjoy seeing you

on Saturday.

I think you

acted very well

I felt like

squeezing you

on the stage.

I tried to fly
when I got
home but I
could not.
It looked lovely
to fly.
Best love and
kisses from
++++++ Nancy ++++++
++++

Fay Compton as Peter Pan
which she played in the
thirteenth revival, New
Theatre, 24 December
1917. Reproduced from a
contemporary magazine.

Bentworth
Alton
Hants

Dear Peter Pan
         We are so sorry
we cannot come to Ports-
mouth to see you as we
did last time you came.
Please dear Peter will
you write and tell us
how to fly. We have
tried so hard and we
keep the window
open for you every
night. Has Wemdy
come to do the spring
cleaning yet. With
love and a thimble From
Ray   Avis Saxton

Postcard, from a watercolour by Barham.

Nina Boucicault, as Peter Pan
in the original production,
Duke of York's Theatre,
27 December 1904. Drawing by
Ralph Cleaver, reproduced from
The Sketch, 4 January 1905.

PETER PAN,

OR

THE BOY WHO WOULDN'T GROW UP.

By J. M. Barrie.

DUKE OF YORK'S THEATRE, LONDON.

		1909.	1908	1907.	1906.	1905.	1904.
Peter Pan...		Pauline Chase	Pauline Chase	Pauline Chase	Pauline Chase	Cecilia Loftus	Nina Boucicault
Mr. Darling		Walter Pearce	Reginald Owen	A. E. Matthews	Marsh Allen	Gerald du Maurier	Gerald du Maurier
Mrs. Darling		Sybil Carlisle	Sybil Carlisle	Sybil Carlisle	Sybil Carlisle	EnidSpencer-Brunton	Dorothea Baird
Wendy Moira Angelo Darling...		Hilda Trevelyan	Gertrude Lang	Hilda Trevelyan	Hilda Trevelyan	Hilda Trevelyan	Hilda Trevelyan
John Napoleon Darling ..		Harry Duff	George Hersee	George Hersee	George Hersee	George Hersee	George Hersee
Michael Nicholas Darling		Herbert Hollom	Herbert Hollom	Herbert Hollom	Ernest Hollom	Harry Edwin Duff	Winifred Geoghegan
Nana		Edward Sillward	Edward Sillward	Edward Sillward	Edward Sillward	Arthur Lupino	Arthur Lupino
Tinker Bell		Jane Wren	Jane Wren	Jane Wren	Jane Wren	Jane Wren	Jane Wren
Tootles ...		Dorothy Minto	Dorothy Minto	Faith Celli	Joan Burnett	Joan Burnett	Joan Burnett
Nibs ...	Members	Nellie Bowman	Nellie Bowman	Nellie Bowman	Nellie Bowman	Christine Silver	Christine Silver
Slightly ...	of	A. W. Baskcomb	A. W. Baskcomb	A. W. Baskcomb	A. W. Baskcomb	A. W. Baskcomb	A. W. Baskcomb
Curly ...	Peter's	Gertrude Lang	Irene Clarke	Winifred Geoghegan	Winifred Geoghegan	Winifred Geoghegan	Alice Du Barry
1st Twin ...	Band	Dagmar Wiehe	May Kinder	Violet Hollom	Maie Ash	Pauline Chase	Pauline Chase
2nd Twin ...		Bertha Stewart	Ivy Knight	Phyllis Embury	Phyllis Embury	Phyllis Beadon	Phyllis Beadon
Jas. Hook The Pirate Captain		Robb Harwood	Robb Harwood	Robb Harwood	Gerald du Maurier	Gerald du Maurier	Gerald du Maurier
Smee ...		George Shelton	George Shelton	George Shelton	George Shelton	George Shelton	George Shelton
Gentleman Starkey		Charles Trevor	Charles Trevor	Charles Trevor	Charles Trevor	Ben Field	Sydney Harcourt
Cookson ...		Charles Medwin	Charles Medwin	Charles Medwin	Charles Medwin	Charles Medwin	Charles Trevor
Cecco ...		Frederick Annerley	William Luff	William Luff	Frederick Annerley	Frederick Annerley	Frederick Annerley
Mullins ...	Pirates	Chris. Walker	Chris. Walker	Chris. Walker	Chris. Walker	Chris. Walker	Hubert Willis
Jukes ...		James English	James English	James English	James English	James English	James English
Noodler ...		John Kelt	John Kelt	John Kelt	John Kelt	John Kelt	John Kelt
			Messrs. Malvern, Saker, and Spencer	Messrs. Malvern, Barry, and Spencer			
Great Big Little Panther Red-		Humphrey Warden	Humphrey Warden	Humphrey Warden		Benson Kleve	Philip Darwin
Tiger Lily ... skins		Margaret Fraser	Margaret Fraser	Mary Mayfren	Mary Mayfren	Mary Mayfern	Miriam Nesbitt
Mermaid ...		———	Marjorie Moore	Norah Dwyer	Gladys Herries	Rosamund Bury	———
Baby Mermaid ...		———	Beryl St. Leger	Tessie Parke	Edith Delevanti	Geraldine Wilson	
Liza ... Author of the Play		Tessie Parke	Tessie Parke	DorothyLemarchand	DorothyLemarchand	Ela Q. May	Ela Q. May

Chart showing the casts in
Peter Pan from 1904 until 1909
in the London productions.